CHANCELLORSVILLE

THE MACMILLAN BATTLE BOOKS ARE PREPARED UNDER
THE GENERAL EDITORSHIP OF EDWARD R. SAMMIS

Bruce Palmer

CHANCELLORSVILLE

DISASTER IN VICTORY

THE MACMILLAN COMPANY, NEW YORK
COLLIER-MACMILLAN LIMITED, LONDON

The Macmillan Company, New York
Collier-Macmillan Canada, Ltd., Toronto, Ontario
Library of Congress catalog card number: 67-17212
Printed in the United States of America
FIRST PRINTING

Maps by Rafael Palacios

PICTURE CREDITS: Confederate Memorial Museum, Richmond, Virginia, 87; Culver Pictures, title page, 14-15, 38-39, 42-43, 50, 56-57, 58, 59, 68-69, 83; Historical Pictures Service-Chicago, 19, 37, 44 (left), 49, 60, 71, 79; Library of Congress, 8-9, 11, 12, 18, 20-21, 22, 24-25, 27, 30, 46-47, 61, 76-77, 80; Radio Times Hulton Picture Library, 13, 16, 31, 32, 35, 44 (right), 64, 90-91. Cover illustration, Culver pictures. Picture research by Patricia Crum.

For Mark and Matthew

CONTENTS

Part One

PLANS for BATTLE
North and South

New Year's Day, 1863

The Rebel soldiers huddled against the cold in makeshift huts and waited, saving themselves for the battle to come. Their officers stared anxiously at the snow-filled clouds that hung over the fortified slopes at Fredericksburg, Virginia. What would the weather and the new year bring?

On December 13, 1862, Union General Ambrose Burnside had blundered to defeat while attacking Fredericksburg, wasting his Army of the Potomac in a costly assault and a futile shift along the banks of the Rappahannock River. He had gotten hopelessly bogged down in mud. But men and supplies were now being drawn together for another Union offensive into Virginia. Could the Confederates be sure of resisting the Federals again?

As the year 1863 began, the Confederacy needed a genuine Southern victory, a bold stroke that would restore the once-bright prospects for independence that had dimmed in the weary year and a half of fighting since the beginning of the Civil War. If the Army of the Potomac could be annihilated and Lincoln's western forces swept from Mississippi and Tennessee, then the Parliament of England might be encouraged by the beleaguered Confederate states to come to their rescue. The mills of England needed Southern cotton. If the Confederate armies won on land, the British Royal Navy could free the South's ports which were currently blockaded by patrolling squadrons of Union warships. The

Southern states had declared their independence two years before; now they must prove to the Union and to the world that they could maintain that independence against heavy odds.

True, General Robert E. Lee's valiant Army of Northern Virginia had turned back Union forces led by Generals McDowell, Pope, McClellan, and, most recently, Burnside. But an overwhelming victory might prove the hinge of triumph on which the door of independence for the Confederacy would swing open forever. It was time now for a daring gamble.

Lincoln Names a New Commander

Confederate civilians, generals, and politicians were guilty of underestimating President Lincoln. Despite frequent disappointment, his view never wavered. "A house divided

A view of the town of Fredericksburg, Virginia, in 1863

General Joseph Hooker, commander of the Army of the Potomac

against itself cannot stand," he had said. Whatever happened, Lincoln intended to fight to the finish and reunite the broken nation. He accepted the resignation of General Burnside and sent a telegram:

January 26, 1863

MAJOR GENERAL JOSEPH HOOKER

General:

I have placed you at the head of the Army of the Potomac. . . . I believe you to be a brave and skillful soldier. . . . What I now ask of you is military success. . . . Beware of rashness, but with energy, and sleepless vigilance, go forward and give us victories.

Yours very truly,
A. Lincoln

Lincoln did not ask advice from anyone in his Cabinet or out of it when he appointed Joseph E. Hooker commander of the Army of the Potomac. The President knew that the man who flaunted the nickname "Fighting Joe" was quarrelsome and ambitious. Worse, he had a reputation as a heavy drinker. Regis de Trobriand, a French-born brigade commander, commented that when whiskey had loosened Hooker's tongue "he indulged in boastings that one hearing could not accept as gospel truth, or reckon modesty in the number of his virtues."

But Hooker had proven himself many times over as a bold corps commander, a leader of several divisions. Lincoln trusted him. From the time he assumed command, Hooker reported directly to Lincoln and received all his instructions from the President.

A Willing Horse with a New Rider

The Army of the Potomac was a sturdy, valiant creature, the muscle, blood, and bone of all the states that had remained within the Union. For two years, this war horse had been ridden hard, sometimes well, sometimes foolishly. The new general's nickname was one to inspire confidence. Once in the saddle, Hooker proved to be an admirable master.

A photograph of "Fighting Joe" in front of a Union army tent

Hooker had genuine talents at organizing. For the first time since its formation, the Army of the Potomac was decently and regularly housed and fed. Hooker insisted on the routines of sanitation, and devoted time, money, and personal interest to the wounded and ill. He dismissed officers he considered disloyal and trained the men with care. If he believed that an army should be "as comfortable and contented as circumstances . . . allow," the general also stated that idleness was "the great evil of all armies. Every effort was made to keep the troops employed; and whenever weather would permit it, they were engaged in field exercises."

All of the new commander's efforts had the desired effect. The Union soldiers soon forgot their humiliating defeat at Fredericksburg when Burnside led them. Major General

Darius Couch, a corps commander and no admirer of Hooker, admitted that he had never before known men "to change from a condition of the lowest depression to that of a healthy fighting state." By the time the muddy roads of Virginia began to dry, the army was ready to be guided into battle again.

During a review, Hooker spoke with pride. Turning to a group of newspaper correspondents, he said, "If the enemy does not run, God help them."

Lee's Record

General Robert E. Lee had assumed command of the Confederate Army of Northern Virginia midway in 1862. As

Soldiers of the Army of the Potomac on a winter campaign

the new year turned, he could look back on the months past with satisfaction. Teamed with the brilliant Virginian corps commander, General T. J. "Stonewall" Jackson, the Confederate forces had fought no less than thirteen battles, great and small, including Mechanicsville, Malvern Hill, Second Manassas (or Second Bull Run, as the Federals called it), bloody Sharpsburg, and the bitter encounter at Fredericksburg that closed the campaigning of 1862. Thirteen battles in seven months, and the Rebels had won eleven times.

Moreover, the lean, hard-driving Southerners had inflicted 70,725 casualties and had seized 75,000 rifles, which they needed desperately. With a loss of only eight cannon, they had captured 155. How many more times would they have to win before the Yankees gave up their stubborn attempts to invade Virginia? How many battles did it take to win a war?

General Robert E. Lee, commander of the Army of Northern Virginia

Every officer in broken boots on a jaded horse, every skinny soldier in threadbare pants and slouch hat could answer those questions. They all knew that the Union could replace every one of the blue-clad soldiers killed, wounded, or taken prisoner. They all knew that the Northern factories and forges could turn out a dozen rifles and six cannon for every one lost in the woods of embattled Virginia. Spies told of warehouses across the Rappahannock bulging with supplies and ammunition, of sprawling corrals filled with horses and mules. And there seemed to be no end of Northerners who volunteered or were drafted into the Federal armies.

Hooker's Strategy—"My Plans Are Perfect"

General Hooker set himself to solve a serious, even dangerous problem. He must do what no commander before him had done: cross the rivers of Virginia in the face of an alert enemy at a point where a fight could be forced on favorable ground. He had learned under Burnside that a crossing too close to Fredericksburg was an invitation to disaster. He had no intention of repeating Burnside's error of piecemeal assault that merely wasted well-trained troops. Lincoln cautioned Hooker, "In your next battle *put in all your men.*" Put them in where? Not below Fredericksburg to the east, for the Rappahannock River was too wide to be bridged.

Hooker soon showed that he could draw up superior programs of swift assault. He had strengthened General George Stoneman's Union cavalry to 10,000 men and proposed to send them slashing into Lee's rear to destroy the scanty Confederate supplies and cut the Rebel communications with Richmond, the Confederate capital. As this was being done, five corps led by Generals Sickles, Couch, Slocum, Meade,

Federal cannon across the Rappahannock from Fredericksburg

and Howard, would cross the broad river to the west, *above* Fredericksburg. Lee, heavily outnumbered, would be forced to retreat toward Richmond. The powerful Union cavalry would check this withdrawal, and Hooker's main army would spring the trap.

Lincoln heartily approved of the plan. The primary objective was very clear: not another clumsy thrust at Richmond, but rather the destruction of the Army of Northern Virginia. Hooker planned simply to follow and harry, pursue, and finally defeat his Southern opponent.

The President wrote enthusiastically, "Pitch into him!" Hooker replied smugly, "My plans are perfect."

Earthworks and Empty Bellies

While Hooker gathered and outfitted his army across the Rappahannock, Lee ordered the rain- and snow-soaked earth of Virginia on the south bank of the river to be heaped up in ramparts. Twenty-five miles of dirt were piled high from

Bank's Ford to Port Royal. Bombproof dugouts were constructed, and rifle pits were dug. The work was hard on men weakened with disease and hampered by bad weather, but it had to be done. Fredericksburg was exposed to Union cannon fire and was already badly damaged.

Another Union force had been reported gathering at the Virginia seaport of Newport News. Lee reluctantly sent off two fine divisions under Generals Longstreet and Pickett to block a possible Federal amphibious assault on Richmond, expressing regrets to Confederate President Jefferson Davis that the loss of these soldiers would mean he could not undertake an offensive later in the spring. Already Lee's thoughts were on Maryland and Pennsylvania, the rich farm lands of the North, a prime target for a prolonged thrust into Union territory. He wanted to carry the war into Federal soil, perhaps to cause Abraham Lincoln to consider peace.

Confederate scouts watched the Army of the Potomac, and

A Civil War cavalry skirmisher (drawing by Edwin Forbes)

the Southern general wrote to one of his daughters, "General Hooker . . . runs out his guns, starts wagons and troops up and down the river and creates an excitement generally. Our men look on in wonder, give a cheer and all subsides." Lee's tone was light, joking, but he was a worried man.

As the weary weeks stretched out, the shortage of food for the men and animals of the Confederate army grew far more serious than Hooker's field exercises. The frozen fields around Fredericksburg had been picked down to stubble and mud, and more than a thousand horses and mules were in winter quarters in North Carolina and far-off Louisiana. Unless the supply of fodder could be increased, the Rebel artillery would be paralyzed, all their captured guns useless. And General Jeb Stuart's cavalry, already at half strength and scattered across the country, would have to be converted into foot soldiers.

Provisions, blankets, medicine, and ammunition were shipped up from Richmond to the Rappahannock fortifications on a single-track railroad. A few wheezy locomotives and odd lots of splintered, worn-out freight cars rattled back and forth, trying to feed an army of 60,000 cold, hungry men.

LEFT TO RIGHT: *Union Generals Henry Slocum, John Sedgwick, Oliver O. Howard, George Meade*

Lee's soldiers and officers suffered from frostbite and scurvy. They wrapped their feet in torn blankets and grubbed in the woods for sassafras buds and wild onions. Their rations were pitifully small. Lee noted, with mounting concern, that "one-fourth pound of bacon, eighteen ounces of flour and ten pounds of rice were issued to each one hundred men" every three days!

To still the gnawing pangs of hunger, the Rebel soldiers attended religious meetings and band concerts. They peered cautiously across the river at something new—observation balloons tugging at anchor ropes, riding in the tattered clouds high above the Union lines.

While the Confederates waited and hungered, the Federal forces watched them from the skies, planned to strike them, and drilled, drilled, drilled.

Mud and a Change of Plans

On April 26, 1863, Hooker ordered out Stoneman's cavalry. The mounted raiders lunged off into sweeping rainstorms. In three days, the cavalry moved only twenty-five miles over

General Stoneman's cavalry assembling to cross the Rappahannock

the mired roads, while their commander fumed and fretted. Hooker pored over maps and changed his original plan. The new plan he relayed to Lincoln showed signs of genuine brilliance.

Hooker now decided to leave 24,000 men behind under the command of capable General John M. Sedgwick, who would threaten Fredericksburg, holding Lee's army there. The main body of the Union force—three strong corps under Generals Meade, Slocum, and Howard—would loop up the Rappahannock some thirty miles, cross, and come down along the south bank on the Confederate side of the river, rendering Lee's earthworks useless and freeing Bank's Ford for Sedgwick to cross. The joint forces would act like two jaws of a great vise. Lee would not merely be caught, but crushed between the jaws.

Springtime and Spies

It rained much more than usual that spring, and the first green shoots for the Confederate horses to crop floated in acres of gluey mud.

Since he had no observation balloons, and his scouts often confused their reports gathered at long distance, Lee relied on a network of spies behind the Union lines. On April 26, Lee wrote to Stonewall Jackson, who commanded his II Corps, "I think that if a real attempt is made to cross the river, it will be *above* Fredericksburg."

Lee's spies, while correct about Hooker's movements, exaggerated the size of his force, insisting that he had gathered a frightening total of 150,000 men. Lee did not believe these rumors, but in truth Fighting Joe and his officers counted off 130,378 men and officers of all ranks and duties. Across the river, Lee had barely 62,000—less than half the striking force of his adversary.

Union Cavalry Crosses

The wind finally shifted enough to make the roads passable. General Stoneman's Union horse soldiers pushed across the swollen Rappahannock west of Fredericksburg. A number of them were swept off the deep fords and drowned, while kerosene torches guttered on the night winds. Lee ordered his son, Rooney, to take a detached group off to the southwest with orders to observe and harass, but to avoid any open encounter. Lee was cautious, playing a waiting game.

Hooker had but one word for his attacking cavalry and he repeated it: "Fight! Fight! Fight!"

Part Two

ADVANCE and ANXIETY

Federal Advance

On the foggy morning of April 29, prolonged cannon fire boomed and muttered across the Rappahannock River, a demonstration designed to pin the Confederates behind their earthen ramparts at Fredericksburg. Up river, Federal engineers quietly and quickly assembled pre-built pontoon bridges across the river. The Union advance guard crossed to the southern bank and secured the bridgehead at Kelly's Ford before the Confederate patrols discovered them. So far, Hooker's extensive planning was paying off.

When he was notified, Lee gave no orders to oppose the crossing. Stoneman's Federal cavalry had crossed and promptly disappeared. This new force might be no more than a diversion while Hooker launched the main blow at another spot. Lee waited.

Despite the heavy rains that had flooded the banks and tributary streams that fed the Rappahannock, 14,000 Union infantry, some guns, and several squadrons of cavalry crossed the river before noon. Jeb Stuart's Confederates watched and counted, waiting for the Yankees to move. Not a shot was fired.

The Union officers had expected resistance at the bridgehead and at the fords. In early afternoon they spread skirmish lines out into the damp underbrush and cleared the bankside. After a pause for regrouping, the advance units wheeled around to face east. Orders were issued to bring over the bulk of three army corps.

At this point, Fighting Joe Hooker was bursting with confidence. He boasted, "The Rebel army is now the legitimate property of the Army of the Potomac."

Still Lee did nothing. In mid-afternoon, Lee's telegraph key chattered: Stuart's cavalry scouts had run down several bands of Union skirmishers and taken prisoners from the V, XI, and XII Corps of the Army of the Potomac. The Union advance was moving steadily toward Ely's Ford on the Rapidan River.

This was serious. An advance by three full corps was not a feint or diversion, but a mass assault. The Confederate commander ordered Stuart back to headquarters.

The telegraph key jumped again, flashing Lee's orders to General R. H. Anderson to face his division left and move it forward, directly into the path of the Union advance. Lee also notified his government in Richmond of the situation at the Rappahannock River and asked for reinforcements.

The soggy skies, threatening all day, broke at twilight, and a drenching rain poured down. The Army of the Potomac halted for the night.

Hammer and Anvil

Lee rode forward early the next day, swinging at an easy trot on his horse, Traveller, to join with the commander of the Confederate II Corps, General T. J. "Stonewall" Jackson.

Stonewall had earned his nickname while fighting on the defensive near the muddy river called Bull Run, the site of the first major battle of the war between the divided states. There the Confederates had rallied behind his Virginia brigade that stood as firm as a stone wall. Since that day, Jackson had proved to be a master of attack, carefully coordinating

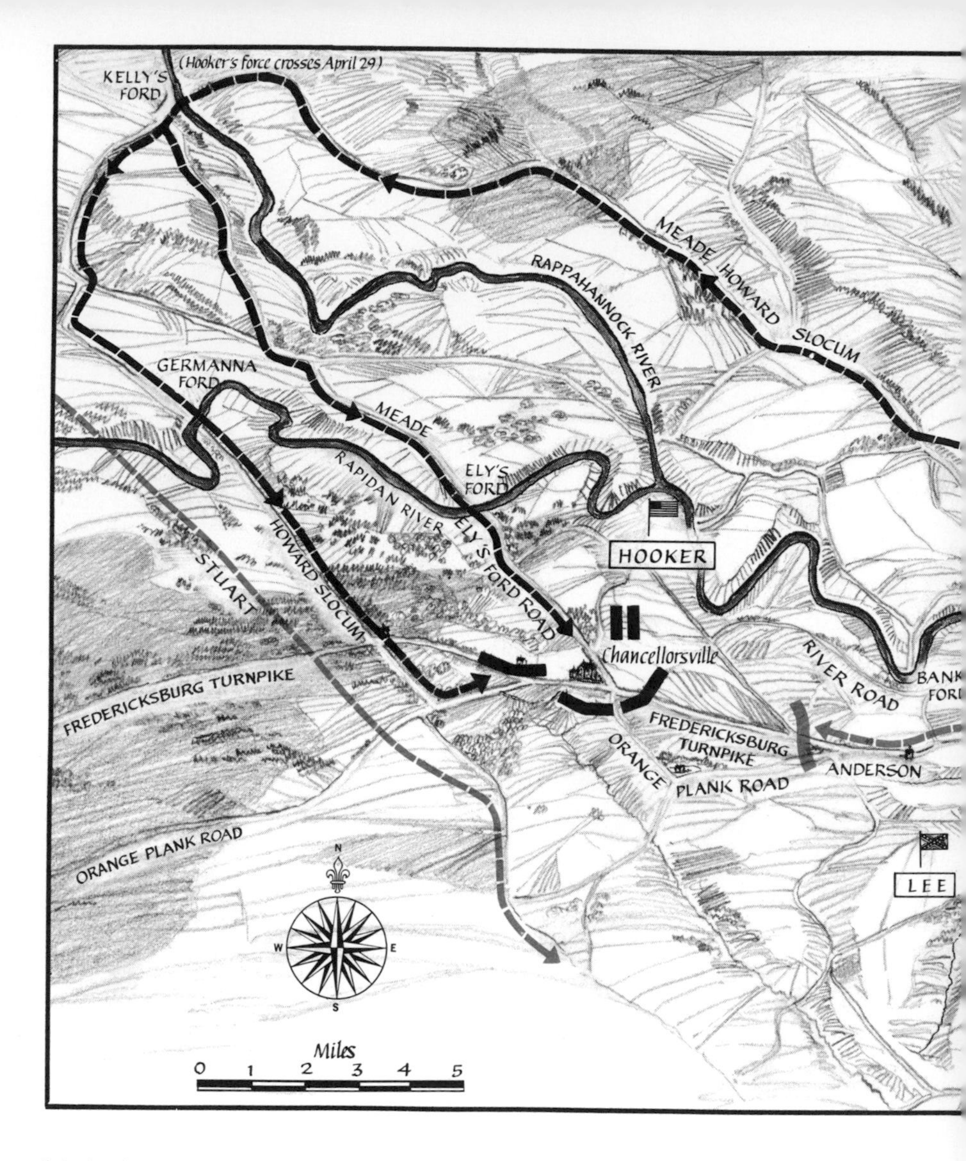

his bold maneuvers with Lee. Jackson had been the hammer, Lee the anvil. Lee held, while Jackson swung and battered Union armies into fragments.

The blue-eyed Jackson was idolized by the soldiers he led and the civilians he protected from Federal invasion. The proudest men in Confederate gray uniforms called themselves the Stonewall Brigade. In Richmond, the Southern capital, one lady commented, "Down here, we sleep securely, with

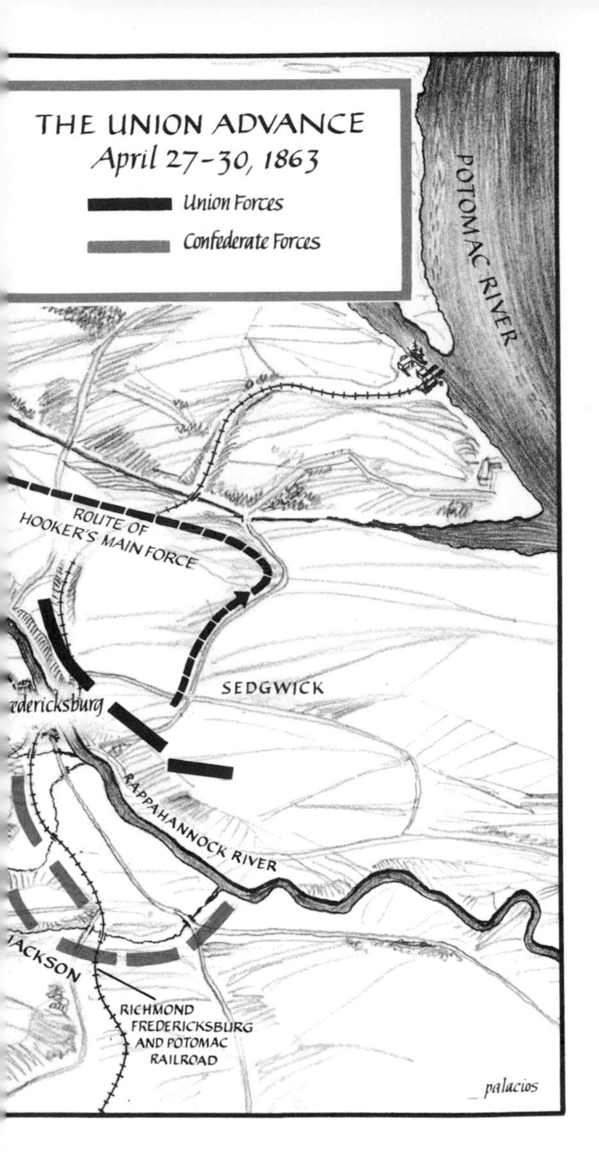

the serenest faith that Stonewall is to flank everybody, and never to be flanked himself." Furious assault on the side, or flank, was the system Jackson had used repeatedly to smash the Yankees. Mrs. Chesnut, in her well-known *Diary from Dixie*, expressed all the Southern faith in this stern Virginia Presbyterian: "Don't you see this Stonewall, how he fires the soldiers' hearts? He fights to win, God bless him! And he *wins!*"

General Thomas J. Jackson, commander of the Confederate II Corps

Not surprisingly, when the two Confederate generals met, Jackson promptly offered to direct an attack. Lee was against this, at least for the present, despite the fact that still more Union troops had crossed into Virginia during the night. Jackson asked for time to consider and rode off on his mount Little Sorrell to study the terrain with his staff officers. Lee waited and watched, then rode to General R. H. Anderson who now faced the Federal columns.

Anderson was a good fighter but slow to start. His division was exposed and weak. He demanded reinforcements at once, but Lee declined to provide any, although he was soon to change his mind. Lee had another plan first.

At 2:30 P.M. on April 30, Lee ordered, for the first time in the military history of the continent of North America, the construction of field fortifications. Anderson's men were to go under cover in open territory. Back in the Revolutionary War, British and American troops had employed earthworks to defend key cities, ports, and river fords, just as Lee had done during the winter along the Rappahannock banks. But this was different, a field force ordered to give up the possibility of rapid movement, to dig and be ready to fight.

At the time, Lee seemed unaware of the historic nature of his decision, but that order was to change the nature of warfare all over the world. Lee had invented trench warfare.

Retreat or Reinforce?

The ground he stood on was Lee's native state. He had pledged his sword and his honor to defend Virginia's soil from Yankee invasion and occupation. Lee was a man of unshakable honesty, a man of his word. Yet he considered ordering a full-scale retreat.

Confederate General Robert H. Anderson

A retreat would be easy and safe. The only apparent alternative was to assault with Anderson's troops, one division against three army corps, impossible odds of at least five to one. Anderson would be wasted, his soldiers sent to slaughter with no chance whatever of success. Reinforce them then.

But this would mean pulling the men off the earthwork defense line at Fredericksburg, stripping the ramparts. Union General Sedgwick, with his observation balloons, could not fail to notice. The whole right side of the Confederate army would be so weakened as to be exposed for a potential deathblow.

Then retreat. But might not Hooker reasonably hope for, even plan on a Confederate withdrawal? It was very possible to back into a trap, to retreat right into the sabers and snipers of the Union cavalry.

But suppose the reinforcements moved at night, when the

A corps of Rebel infantry on a night march

Union balloonists could see nothing; if support could be sent to Anderson without the knowledge of the Yankees? Lee nodded and dictated a rapid stream of orders. He would throw more troops in with Anderson under cover of darkness and hope that Stonewall Jackson could devise a scheme to surprise the powerful Union army.

Confederate General Lafayette McLaws, stationed with his division at Fredericksburg, had been warned earlier to stand by. He was now ordered to move his men directly west, starting at midnight. Jackson would follow at dawn with most of the II Corps. Both generals were to join Anderson.

Moonlight March

Like a silver ship, the new moon sailed over the rain-washed woods west of Fredericksburg. McLaws's infantry wrapped their canteens and bayonets in their shirts to keep them from rattling. They knotted laces and slung their shoes around their necks, not so much for silence as to save a soaking.

Soft orders passed from post to post. The men rose up by companies and stepped out onto the rain-softened roads. Cool, gritty mud oozed between their toes. Officers on horseback clumped by. Another series of whispered commands. The gray columns ghosted forward.

Off slightly to the north and east, Stonewall Jackson and his division commander of North Carolina infantry, A. P. Hill, were already awake and stirring. Two days' rations had been cooked and dry ammunition issued, sure signs of hot action ahead.

McLaws marched his men at a fast pace under the brilliant moon. Night birds called *whip-poor-will, whip-poor-will* and suddenly hushed as the men paced by. A horse snuffled and stamped. Fog drifted down, light tendrils at first, through the dripping trees, shrouding the divisions of Jackson and Hill that followed the Turnpike west.

Jackson left a division behind at Fredericksburg—10,000 men and forty-five guns under General Jubal Early. As the II Corps of the Confederate army marched, Lee's force split quietly into two unequal parts.

"I Know Nothing of This Ground!"

General Hooker's 70,000 veterans pushed steadily east toward Fredericksburg. The invasion of Virginia had worked perfectly thus far. Hooker had the double advantage of position and power. He could hit and hit hard, uncover Bank's Ford, overrun the thinned Fredericksburg earthworks, and scatter Lee's Confederate force into the tangled, heavy forest called The Wilderness.

Hooker pondered over maps until he grew weary and short-tempered. The Union cavalry under General Stoneman seemed to have vanished into the Virginia woods. Fighting Joe began to think that he was groping blindly. He grew increasingly nervous. One historian has written of Hooker, "He had difficulty in coordinating the movements of bodies of troops whose positions he could judge only by reports. . . . He lacked the iron resolution required in a great battle captain."

All Hooker had to do was drive on, uncover the ford, and bring across Sedgwick's force. His corps commanders expected him to do this. Instead, he slowed the speed of the advance, moved his scouts out, and ordered shallow rifle pits and gun emplacements to be dug. He sweated and scribbled in his tent, shuffling his maps and worrying about the location of his

Yankee artillerymen manning a mortar (photograph by Gardiner)

artillery. He turned to General Gouverneur K. Warren of his staff and said bitterly, "My God . . . I know nothing of this ground!" Abruptly, Hooker ordered his powerful army to halt. Fighting Joe abandoned the initiative he had so brilliantly seized and went on the defensive.

Hooker did not even place his own divisions, but left that to Warren and his staff. Nervous, baffled by the terrain—miles of thick forest cut with narrow, poorly surfaced roads—the Union commander merely indicated a spot that marked a crossroads, not even a town really, just a few houses and outbuildings where two roads, the Orange Plank Road and the Turnpike, crossed near John Chancellor's square red farmhouse. The spot on the map was called Chancellorsville.

Lee Breaks the Rules

Lee's decision to split his army was a desperate gamble, a clear violation of one of the most important unwritten rules by which men wage war. The rule is that a general with a small army does not divide his weak force in the face of a more numerous, powerful enemy. If he does, he merely offers himself for conquest. But Lee deliberately broke this rule. And he meant to win, not lose.

Just as the first weakness of Anderson's exposed division encouraged Lee to introduce trench warfare, the lack of reinforcements urged him to abandon traditional tactics. The Army of Northern Virginia had to be in two places at once, facing both Sedgwick and Hooker. Early would hold at Fredericksburg, while the rest of the army smashed at Hooker. Split in two, the Confederates would have to stand toe-to-toe with the veteran Union infantry and slug it out. By surprise attack (always attack; his orders never contemplated defense) Lee meant to break the closer, more massive jaw of Hooker's iron vise.

Lee rode down the Orange Plank Road. He caught up with Stonewall Jackson, just as the first skirmishers from McLaws' and Anderson's divisions exploded into a fire fight with Union pickets. Both men trotted on toward the battle that had begun to sputter in the damp, tangled woods.

Jackson was dressed in full uniform, a gift to him from admiring Confederate civilians for his audacious and successful campaign in the Shenandoah Valley, a series of lightning assaults that had made him famous. Lee seemed plain by contrast, but this was not unusual; the modest Confederate commander seldom wore the dress uniform and maroon sash of rank.

As the two men rode, wave after wave of cheering broke from the throats of the Virginia brigades, the Alabama troops, the tough Georgians, and the North Carolina infantry. Here were two generals who did not boast of victories, but planned and fought together to win them! The cheers crashed like surf for Jackson and for Lee.

First Skirmish—May 1

The gray fighters under McLaws and Anderson did not charge headlong at the Union army. Skirmishers and sharpshooters sniped at each other as they skidded, clambered, and sprawled in the snaggy second-growth timber. The Federals

Skirmishers open fire in the woods near Chancellorsville.

May 1, 1863: General Hooker's forces forming into battle line at Chancellorsville clearing (drawing by Alfred R. Waud)

gave ground slowly but steadily, dodging back over the fallen trees and skirting the boggy swamps. Wild dogwood and flowers bloomed everywhere in the thick woods. The few wounded prisoners taken by Anderson's advance were from General George Meade's Yankee V Corps. Grateful to their captors for the medical attention given to them before they were herded to the rear, the Yankees admitted that they really didn't know where they were. They had just followed "those Dutchmen" across the Rapidan River.

"Those Dutchmen" had brigade leaders named Von Gilsa, Dachrodt, Von Amberg, Bushbeck, and Schimmelfennig—not Dutch, but *Deutsch*, German-Americans commanded by pious General O. O. Howard. This was the Union XI Corps,

regiment after regiment of broad-shouldered, tough bluecoats—farmers and blacksmiths. Many of these men spoke imperfect English, and orders were given to them in German.

Hooker had decided that it would not be smart or safe to use Howard's "foreign" troops at the center of attack or defense. It was easy enough for orders to get twisted under any sort of battle conditions. What might happen when a breathless courier shouted something in the din of combat to a group of German-speaking officers and men, and then galloped off into the dim forest again?

In order to avoid confusion and possible disaster, Hooker had ordered his staff officers to place Howard's XI Corps on the far right flank, far away from the presumed center of the coming conflict. Later in the battle they might do for reserve troops in a mopping-up action.

Hooker was now in an ideal position. Lee's staff was aware only that there was a very large Union force (estimated correctly by the Confederates as 70,000 men) in and around the crossroads and Mr. Chancellor's square red house. It seemed very likely that, with so many men, Hooker could use one whole corps to construct a great living screen behind which other divisions could maneuver to explode suddenly out through the tangled, dripping trees. It would not be hard for the Yankee commander to adjust the jaws of his great crushing vise unseen.

The Union Right Flank

After sunset on May 1, Lee learned the approximate position of the Yankee army. But he learned the hard way. General Jeb Stuart's horse artillery had engaged in a running battle along the Union front at dusk. Heavy Federal cannon fire came from Fairview Cemetery, and rifle volley indicated killing concentrations of infantry of General Henry Slocum's XII Corps west of Chancellorsville, where General Daniel Sickles' blue division was dug in along the Orange Plank Road to the Turnpike junction.

Lee and Jackson sat on a fallen pine log and conferred for the second time. Jackson insisted that the Union army could be hurled back across the river the next day. Lee hoped so, but he was less optimistic. He ordered a reconnaissance out to locate and plot the western wing of the Federal force. It seemed to Lee, faced by the hidden masses ahead and to the east, that the Confederate attack would have to be launched from the west. The Union right flank quickly became the most important segment of Hooker's Army of the Potomac.

Howard "Up in the Air"

General O. O. Howard had followed orders. His XI Corps sprawled west, slightly in front of the Orange Plank Road, across the Turnpike intersection. To his left was Sickles' division; to his right was woods. There, in the dense forest, his line ended. Thus Howard's position violated another basic rule of warfare from the time of the Roman Caesars: never attack, halt, or defend with exposed flanks. In any maneuver, a good commander is careful to establish his army in reference to the terrain on which the infantry must move. The weakest parts of any army, at any time and place, are the extreme ends, or flanks. Whenever possible, these loose ends should be anchored to some piece of terrain that will protect against or deflect a sudden enemy assault that might threaten to encircle the army as a whole. A mountain or range of hills offers a natural vantage point for long-range observation, as well as shelter. A lake or swamp will force an attacker miles out of his way. A flank should never end with soldiers strung out in an open field or, worse, in a forest that can conceal an enemy attack.

Not many of Howard's junior officers were widely experienced. They had allowed their German-speaking soldiers to halt and make camp where it was convenient. No blue cavalry patrolled the woods beyond them. The Union right flank was anchored to nothing at all. It was "up in the air."

Before midnight, Jeb Stuart rode into Lee's casual headquarters camp with great news. He had discovered "those Dutchmen."

That settled it. Now Lee knew the approximate position of Hooker's entire army from east to west. He and Jackson studied their maps. Both men knew that there were a number of trails and cart tracks cutting through the woods that had never been indicated on any map. Lee traced a fourteen-mile semicircle that ended on the exposed Union XI Corps. Then he leaned back and mused, "How can we get at these people?"

Jackson offered to find out. In his staff he numbered a clergyman who had once been minister of a local church, and an officer of engineers, a specialist in maps, bridges, and roads. He would check and submit a detailed plan. With a final promise to move at dawn, Jackson left his commander to snatch a few hours' badly needed sleep.

Major Hotchkiss and Mr. Lacy Find a Road

Silence settled over the pine thickets. Weary soldiers in both armies tried to sleep on the damp sod. Jackson's men—

the engineer, Major Hotchkiss, and the clergyman, Mr. Lacy—prowled off through the dark, looking for a route for the proposed Confederate attack.

Jackson slept poorly, woke, and shivered by a feeble fire. As he sipped coffee and chatted with an aide, his sword, leaning against a tree, clattered suddenly to the ground, although no one stood within yards of it. While not normally superstitious, the shocked aide took the incident as a bad omen, a prophecy of disaster in the woods.

Confederate headquarters began to stir long before dawn. Lee woke and joined Jackson for breakfast by the fire. Soon Major Hotchkiss and Mr. Lacy returned, excited, and rightly so. They had found a crude road, a little-used cart track, well out of sight of the enemy. This overgrown trail led to a better road that ran, in turn, beyond and behind the enemy right flank. Not only that, but the proprietor of an abandoned

A sketch by Waud showing General O. O. Howard's headquarters and the position of the Union XI Corps on May 2, 1863

LEFT: *Confederate General Ambrose P. Hill.* RIGHT: *General Jeb Stuart, commander of the Confederate cavalry*

ironworks called Catherine Furnace was willing to act as a guide.

Lee turned to his corps commander.

"General Jackson, what do you propose to do?"

"Go around here," Jackson replied, tracing the trail Hotchkiss had marked on the map.

"What do you propose to make this movement with?"

"My whole corps," Jackson said calmly.

That was Jackson's bold contribution to an already daring plan. He would attack the Union right flank from the west, swinging 26,000 men in a hammer blow of such force that the scattered Army of the Potomac would be driven in spinning fragments back to the banks of the Rappahannock River.

Lee was, for once, dumbfounded. Split the army—*again?*

"What will you leave me?" he asked, finally.

"The divisions of Anderson and McLaws."

Two understrength divisions to face an estimated 70,000 men? *Defy the rules of war twice in two days?*

But if the center could hold, solid as an anvil, as it had before, until Jackson fell on the exposed Union right flank . . . Lee took a deep breath and gambled for an overwhelming victory.

"Well," he said calmly, "go on."

Jackson Moves Out—May 2

At 7 A.M., Jackson's columns, brigade after brigade, swung off to the southwest, heading toward the slit of overgrown trail at Catherine Furnace. Jeb Stuart's artillery went with them, and A. P. Hill detached some of his division for a rear guard to shield the baggage trains. The roads were neither dusty nor muddy. No telltale clouds rose to warn the Union army; no thick mire clotted the wheels and axles of gun carriages or ammunition caissons. 26,000 men were swallowed up by the dense, dripping forest.

Lee watched Jackson move out with mingled admiration and confidence. A few days later, he remarked, "Such an executive officer the sun never shone on. I have but to show him my design, and I know that if it can be done, it will be done. Straight as the needle to the pole he advanced to the execution of my purpose."

Part Three

TWO DAYS of BATTLE

"I Should Feel Easy"

The Confederate Army of Northern Virginia was now in three parts: Early with his 10,000 at Fredericksburg; Lee with the divisions of Anderson and McLaws, a scanty 14,000 facing the brutal power of the Union center; and Jackson with the II Corps, 26,000 men, advancing on the Union right. A fourth fragment, two regiments of cavalry detached under Rooney Lee, was still scouting Stoneman's Union raiders southwest of Fredericksburg.

Early's force received careful instructions. First, they were to hold fast if attacked. Second, if the enemy before them reduced forces, Early was to send picked reinforcements to Chancellorsville. Finally, if Sedgwick suddenly disappeared from Fredericksburg, Early was to join Lee at once.

Anderson and McLaws were given desperate duty: hold a front three and one-quarter miles long. Confederate infantrymen were spaced along the line six feet apart—an ominous distance, the length of a grave. This front, so thinly manned, was to be held, with light artillery support, until Jackson launched his attack. No matter what happened, no matter how furious the Federal assaults, the center *must hold*.

Lee was fully conscious of the enormous risks he was taking. This was his second war, for, like many men both north and south who had graduated from West Point Military Academy, Lee had fought in the Mexican War. He was short of men, short of supplies, soon to be short of ammunition.

He sent a dispatch to Confederate President Jefferson Davis that read in part: "If I had with me all my command, I should feel easy, but, as far as I can judge, the advantage of numbers and position is greatly in favor of the enemy."

"Press On!"

East of Howard's exposed XI Corps, the Union line was manner by infantry commanded by General Daniel Sickles, an impulsive man. Word filtered back to his headquarters that some sort of movement was being made by an unidentified Rebel force of unknown size. Some wagons had been sighted moving west. Sickles did not hesitate, but moved his division forward, opening a gap in the Federal line between his force and Howard's corps. Sickles' infantry probed through the heavy woods and ran into A. P. Hill's North Carolina rear guard.

The afternoon wore away with occasional hot exchanges, mostly Federal artillery fire and clashes between Hill's rear guard and Sickles' men.

Union General Daniel Sickles

At Confederate headquarters, Lee's staff officers watched the action at the center, where Anderson and McLaws were under attack. There was no sign of a general Union assault, despite the Yankees' great strength. It seemed as if the blue army was too tightly packed. Units seemed to come into action and then drift back, as though they were getting in each others' way in the hampering underbrush.

There was still no word from Stuart and Jackson. What had happened? Had the Confederate flank attack been discovered and turned back? Why was the promised hammer stroke so long delayed? How long could Anderson and McLaws hold?

Then in mid-afternoon, Lee received a single sheet of paper scrawled on both sides. Jackson informed his commander that the leading division was "up & the next two appear to be well closed." On the back of the sheet, Jeb Stuart had writ-

Union horse artillery going into action

ten, "I will come in on the flank and help all I can when the ball opens." There was nothing for Lee to do but wait.

As the sun dropped in the sky, the suspense rose. Out there to the west, Jackson was urging his men forward, repeating his famous catch phrase: "Press on! Press on!"

Bad News

Then came startling information, bad news—not from the west, but from the east. Somehow, Lee's courier had confused the instructions he relayed. The orders had not been written, out of fear that the rider might be captured by a sudden thrust forward of the Union infantry. General Early had been given to understand that he was to join Lee at once. Although puzzled, even angry, Early had followed what he thought were his orders, stripping the earthworks at Fredericksburg and marching to join Lee. The entire Confederate rear had been thrown open to Sedgwick!

Lee immediately ordered Early to return to Fredericksburg and took care not to alarm the officers and men already in battle. As far as they knew, Early still covered them.

Lee's calm face did not show his inner anxiety. If Sedgwick rushed the Fredericksburg line, if Jackson was ambushed, if Anderson and McLaws broke under the Federal battering . . . Lee swept the thoughts from his mind and rode up to the center. Although exposed to Union artillery fire, he sat there on his horse, steadily discussing the problems of education with a German military observer.

Then, faint at first like distant thunder, came a rumble from the west. The noise rolled across the woods, drowning the rattle of small arms. Across the darkening skies, the fused shells from Stuart's guns streamed into the tangled wilderness and burst in crimson flashes. Seconds later, the sounds of the exploding shells reached Lee's ears. Jackson's attack had begun. "The ball" was open at last!

Dutchmen at Dinner

Completely unaware of Jackson's stealthy advance, the Union infantry commanded by General Howard lounged at ease. They were more than two miles from the nearest action —or so they thought. Even Sickles' lunge forward had not disturbed them. The gap between the XI Corps and Sickles' troops still yawned open. Officers and men had spent a rather dull day, listening to other men fight.

Now their rifles were stacked, fresh-slaughtered beef had been distributed to the company mess cooks, wood gathered, and coffee sat bubbling over the campfires. Here and there the men joked over games of pinochle and skat. The pickets could smell the grilling beef.

West of the Union sentries, the Confederate II Corps spread from the Orange Plank Road north across the Turnpike. Jackson's eyes blazed as he gave the order: *Fix bayonets!*

The Rebel troops lay in close attack formations, two miles of men with long, glittering bayonets that caught the rays of the setting sun. Georgia boys and lean Alabama troops bit cartridges, loaded and cocked their rifles. They knew what sort of men lay beyond them, loafing out the last hours of daylight—"Foreigners," "Dutchers," "bounty boys," believed to be mercenaries, soldiers who fought, not out of conviction or patriotism, but strictly for money. Rumors linked Howard's troops with Hessian soldiers, hated by Americans for their part in the Revolutionary War nearly a century earlier. Of all the Yankees, "bounty boys" were the worst.

Jackson took out his pocket watch and looked at the hands. 5:15 P.M.

"Are you ready?" he asked. "You can go forward then."

Confederate Attack

The bugle call rang through the forest. A signal gun blasted. The underbrush crackled like a forest fire as the gray lines rose and went crashing forward. Ahead of them dashed terrified deer and rabbits. Brigade followed brigade, first at a walk, trying to keep the lines straight, then faster, breaking into a clumsy trot through the tearing briars and around the trees, and finally a full, headlong run.

The startled Union pickets listened to the roar of 26,000 men bearing down on them like a vast gray wave. Scattered shots puffed out in the direction of the noise.

Instantly, without command, thousands of throats raised the high, keening "Rebel yell," the blood-chilling battle cry of Confederate infantry.

The gray throngs burst out of the woods, smashing through the picket positions, howling, firing, stabbing. Campfires were scattered and tents flattened beneath the mass of men. Small knots of Union infantry resisted for a few seconds, fighting with unloaded rifles, before they were crushed beneath the terrible assault. On and on the attackers roared, thrusting their way over the light earthworks at Talley's Farm, then scrambling up the slopes of the low ridge beyond.

Jackson rode in close behind the gray lines. He seemed to observers to be seized in an ecstasy of battle joy. At every wild, victorious cry that floated back from the shot-torn woods, his head jerked up toward the sky in exultation. Again and again he raised his hands in praise and benediction. The shattering blow had fallen.

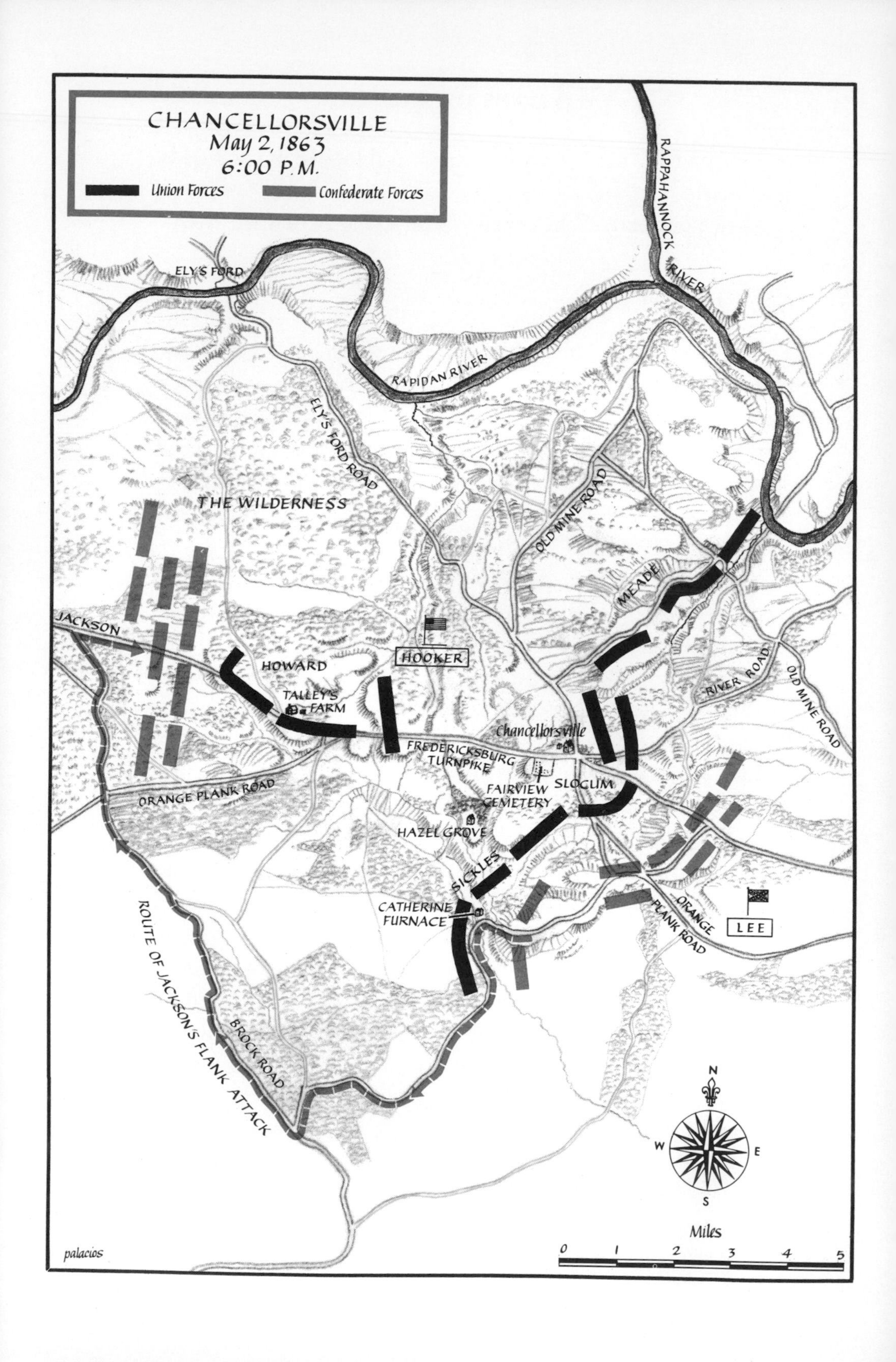
CHANCELLORSVILLE
May 2, 1863
6:00 P.M.
Union Forces
Confederate Forces
ELY'S FORD
RAPPAHANNOCK RIVER
RAPIDAN RIVER
ELY'S FORD ROAD
THE WILDERNESS
OLD MINE ROAD
MEADE
JACKSON
HOOKER
HOWARD
TALLEY'S FARM
RIVER ROAD
OLD MINE ROAD
Chancellorsville
FREDERICKSBURG TURNPIKE
FAIRVIEW CEMETERY
SLOCUM
ORANGE PLANK ROAD
HAZEL GROVE
SICKLES
CATHERINE FURNACE
ORANGE PLANK ROAD
LEE
ROUTE OF JACKSON'S FLANK ATTACK
BROCK ROAD
N
W
E
S
Miles
0 1 2 3 4 5
palacios

"It Was a Running Fight"

One Confederate soldier who broke through the woods on May 2 was Private John O. Casler of the Stonewall Brigade. He wrote later, "We took [Howard's troops] completely by surprise. . . . We ran through the enemy's camps, where they were cooking supper. Tents were standing, and camp-kettles were on the fires full of meat. I saw a big Newfoundland dog lying in one tent as quietly as if nothing had happened. . . . It was a running fight for three miles."

"Those Dutchmen" never had a chance. Survivors of the wrecked XI Corps later gave accounts of a twilight nightmare: hordes of lean, tattered men who came shrieking out of the woods, firing at point-blank range; battered and bleeding blue troopers reeling before an irresistible attack; flames from the scattered campfires spreading through the woods. Here and there, the under-experienced Union soldiers fought back savagely, snatching up stacked rifles and swinging them like clubs, only to fall beneath a rain of bullets. Most of the rest, officers and men, ran headlong in a wild rout, turned and stood for a few seconds, and ran again. Divisions, brigades, and companies spilled together into the gap left by Sickles. Panicked and buffeted, jarred off balance and out of nerve by the fleeing mob of Howard's wrecked corps, Sickles' men wheeled and fired blindly at their own comrades!

Nightfall

In a single instant, the sun seemed to vanish behind the thick trees. The Rebel attackers, who by now had outstripped their own artillery support, floundered blindly in gloom, their own formations suddenly as tangled as the Federals they had stampeded.

Private Casler commented on how quickly the attack, so long delayed, broke down into a "terrible noise and confusion," as Rebels and Yankees cursed and struggled, shot and shouted, trying to form lines and companies.

Sickles' men, after the first turmoil, re-formed in some sort of jumbled order, far enough apart to let Howard's unarmed survivors stream off to safety. Then they fell back, resisting fiercely, to fresh-dug fortifications at Hazel Grove, just west of Chancellorsville.

General Hooker's commander of artillery, Charles Griffin, had placed twenty heavy cannon at Fairview Cemetery. The Federal gunners were veterans, well directed and supplied

with abundant ammunition: solid shot, fused shells, and murderous cannister shot—loose packages of musket balls, the deadliest defense against infantry assault. Griffin's gunners could not see the attacking Rebels, but they could hear the uproar to the west, coming closer and closer. A mob of fleeing Yankees rushed by. Griffin's heavy guns blazed and bucked, flinging short-fused shells and cannister into the darkness, chewing the trees, and smashing into the first Southern attackers.

The Union gunners were blinded by their own muzzle blasts, but fired on and on, tearing the bodies of demoralized Union infantrymen and shocked Confederates alike.

Howard's troops flee in confusion before Jackson's attack.

The night that came too soon, too dark, saved both the reeling Union right wing and Jackson's howling attackers. The blue infantry, though battered and routed in sections, did not break apart completely. Small units stood and fought, gathered stragglers, and made it to the trenches at Hazel Grove. The Rebels broke off their mass, disorganized pursuit and dug shallow "nose holes" with their bare hands and bayonets to hide from the howling shell fragments that sprayed through the trees as Griffin's Union gunners fired irregular salvoes.

General Jackson was the first to recover from the collision. Before this night was over, he meant to fulfill his promise to Lee of a few days earlier: the Yankees would be driven back across the river—those lucky enough to live. If he could collect a sufficient number of his confused command, he meant to hurl them forward once more, this time northeast,

"The Battle of Chancellorsville" (print by Kurz & Allison)

General Sickles' men covering the retreat of the XI Corps

between Chancellorsville and the Rappahannock fords, sealing off any Union retreat to the river. Then, when morning came, the fight would be pushed to the finish: the total destruction of Hooker's army and the capture of the enemy general staff—boots, baggage, and gold braid.

As on the previous night, the new moon rose, but the sky was filled with scattered clouds. As Jackson rode forward to see what could be done to pull the Confederate II Corps into fighting shape, the battle sputtered to life. Yankees and Rebels fired at each others' muzzle flashes. Vicious little hand-to-hand combats continued through the night. The astonished Federals took some prisoners who were stark naked. In the fury of their assault, the captured Rebels had their worn-out uniforms ripped from their bodies by the brambles and briars.

As was his habit, Jackson told no one of his plans until

General Jackson on his fateful ride toward the Rebel lines

9:00 P.M., when he issued a stream of orders, demanding a gathering of his scattered front line and reinforcements from A. P. Hill.

A small cavalcade of staff officers, including his brother-in-law, Lieutenant Morrison, accompanied Jackson as he rode out to the Confederate skirmish lines. In his eagerness to press the advantage to overwhelming triumph, Jackson rode on alone, slightly ahead of his staff.

The troop of riders passed some Rebel pickets, sentries from a lost section of A. P. Hill's North Carolina division. Jackson's officers were fearful, for rumors of Yankee cavalry had already reached them.

"The danger is over. The enemy is routed!" Jackson snapped. "Go back and tell A. P. Hill to press right on!"

Except where moonlight occasionally lit the dark road, nothing could be seen. Jackson paused to ponder the hazards of the night attack. Then he turned and rode back the way he had come.

Suddenly, several shots rang out from the side of the dark road . . . then a volley.

"Cease firing!"

Lieutenant Morrison, closer to Jackson, took up the frantic cry: "You are firing into your own men!"

"It's a lie!" a Southern voice snarled back. "Pour it into them, boys!"

There was a long, low flash in front of Jackson, a volley by a kneeling line. Bullets slammed into the cavalcade of officers and couriers at point-blank range.

Captains Boswell and Forbes were killed, a courier from Stuart's artillery and a Signal Corps sergeant too. Morrison's riddled horse buckled and went down, flinging the young lieutenant into the road. Rearing horses and shouting men spilled together in the dark.

In the same terrible instant, Stonewall Jackson was hit three times.

One ball punctured his right hand, two others struck him in the left arm, tearing his wrist and shattering the bone midway between the elbow and the shoulder.

Somehow, Jackson managed to turn his frightened horse. A low-hanging branch struck him a stunning blow in the face. He reeled in the saddle and collapsed into the arms of one of his aides, Captain Wilbourn.

Stonewall the invincible had been flanked at last, shot down by his own soldiers.

"*It Is a Mere Trifle*"

Captain Wilbourn carried Jackson off the road and set the bleeding commander down beneath a small tree. He stripped off the general's jacket and blood-filled gauntlets, then sent messengers to Stuart and to the corps's skilled medical director, Dr. McGuire. While he waited, Wilbourn bound a kerchief below Jackson's shoulder as a tourniquet to check the flow of blood and rigged a crude sling. Then he asked the general if he had been hit elsewhere.

"In my right hand," Jackson said evenly. "It is a mere trifle."

A litter was finally found, and the wounded general was carried slowly to the rear. Union artillery fire, drawn by the sudden clamor of men and the sound of galloping horses in the dark, swept across the forest. Shells crashed at treetop level. Iron fragments sprayed through the branches. A. P. Hill, Jackson's second-in-command, now in the area to aid in the evacuation, was struck in the leg by a piece of shrapnel and suffered a wound nearly as serious as Jackson's. For a brief time, the two Confederate leaders lay side by side, each concealing from the other the extent of his injury.

The moon filtered through the clouds and lighted Jackson's lacerated brow as he was lifted into the ambulance. Although in great pain and weak from loss of blood, Jackson did not quit the field of battle without a final order. He singled out a number of brigade commanders and insisted, "You must hold your ground."

Surgery

The horse-drawn ambulance jolted slowly to a field hospital located four miles in the rear. A three-man team of surgeons made a careful examination of Jackson's injuries. His left arm was shattered, the wound filled with bone splinters. If Dr. McGuire did not amputate, there would be grave danger of infection, blood poisoning, and gangrene. Jackson gave his permission. Precious chloroform, smuggled into the

Confederacy from England by a blockade runner, was dripped on a cloth cone, and Jackson slipped into pain-free unconsciousness. The surgeons worked quickly.

The operation was successful, and before morning Jackson regained conciousness. His mind was clear enough to recognize the men gathered around him. He gave his formal approval for the order of the morning's action. With Hill badly wounded too, General Jeb Stuart, the thirty-year-old cavalry leader—who had never in his life directed infantry movements—took over as leader of the Confederate II Corps, three-fifths of Lee's army.

Lee Learns the Great and Terrible News

From midnight to the dawn of May 3, 1863, General Slocum's Federal infantry, holding the Union center, listened to the whippoorwills call. Many remembered the curious, eery concert years later.

At 2:30 A.M., Captain Wilbourn, near a state of physical collapse, reached General Lee's headquarters. As well as he could, Wilbourn explained the attack, the territory seized and held, the number of prisoners taken, and the approximate position of the confused Confederate troops. Lee nodded and smiled quietly. But when he learned what had happened on the dark road, the Southern leader could not contain his emotions. He moaned, "Ah, captain, any victory is dearly bought which deprives us of the services of General Jackson even for a short time!"

As word of the disaster spread through the Confederate ranks, many Rebel fighters felt that the birds were singing a monotonous lament, a death dirge for the stricken Stonewall.

Northern artillery in action (photograph by Brady)

Lee accepted the change of command and before dawn ordered Stuart: "Keep the troops well together, and press on . . . by the right wing, turning the positions of the enemy, so as to drive him from Chancellorsville."

Lee himself had taken up the catch phrase of his subordinate: "Press on."

Union Losses— May 3

General O. O. Howard was a deeply religious man, and mourned for his casualties. The Union XI Corps had lost more than 2,000 men in less than two hours' fighting. As a fighting unit, "those Dutchmen" had been destroyed.

General Sedgwick, back across the Rappahannock, was ordered to occupy Fredericksburg, once again defended by Early, then march on Chancellorsville along the Turnpike, taking care to "attack and destroy" any Confederate troop concentrations he encountered en route. Sedgwick supported his engineers with an artillery bombardment. His troops moved promptly. One side of the great vise began to close.

The other jaw had been battered and bent out of position, but not yet broken. There was still a battle to be fought.

On the morning of May 3, Fighting Joe Hooker again held the superior position, better actually than during the previous day. His tightened lines formed a blunt point, or salient, between the two parts of the Confederate army, Stuart's troops and Lee's. Griffin's artillery had proved to be completely effective. From Fairview Cemetery they could shell either Rebel group. Hooker's men and officers were ready to strike; they waited for the order to come from the big, red house by the crossroads. Everything that had been lost could still be won by a full-scale counterattack. Hooker's staff repeatedly urged a massive counterthrust. The salient should be exploited, widened and deepened. First one and then the other piece of the Rebel force could be wrecked, although it was possible to accomplish both tasks at once, if the counterattack used every fighting man. General Couch, always rather short-tempered, announced that a mass assault was merely a "reasonable, common-sense" maneuver.

But Hooker hesitated. Instead of slashing at Lee, he called Sickles back from Hazel Grove, abandoning another position without a fight. A number of Federal officers were furious. Why didn't the general order the counterattack?

Later, Hooker tried to throw the entire blame on Howard's XI Corps, but in his more honest moments, he knew that the fault was his own. He could only say lamely, "I just lost confidence in Joe Hooker."

Confederate Gains

There was no loss of confidence in the gray forces at Sunday daybreak. Lee glared solemnly at the Union salient and resolved to beat his way through the dense blue ranks. Stuart, about two miles away as the crow flies, was to continue the assault from the west. This double drive had to puncture the Federal line and join behind Chancellorsville, sealing off the retreat routes north.

Anderson's and McLaws's divisions were issued fresh ammunition. They crunched slowly straight ahead, through heavy woods filled with scattered, but still-dangerous pockets of Union resistance, the remnants of the XI Corps and some of Sickles' stragglers. Support troops under General Wright pivoted to face north, until they stood closest to Stuart's men.

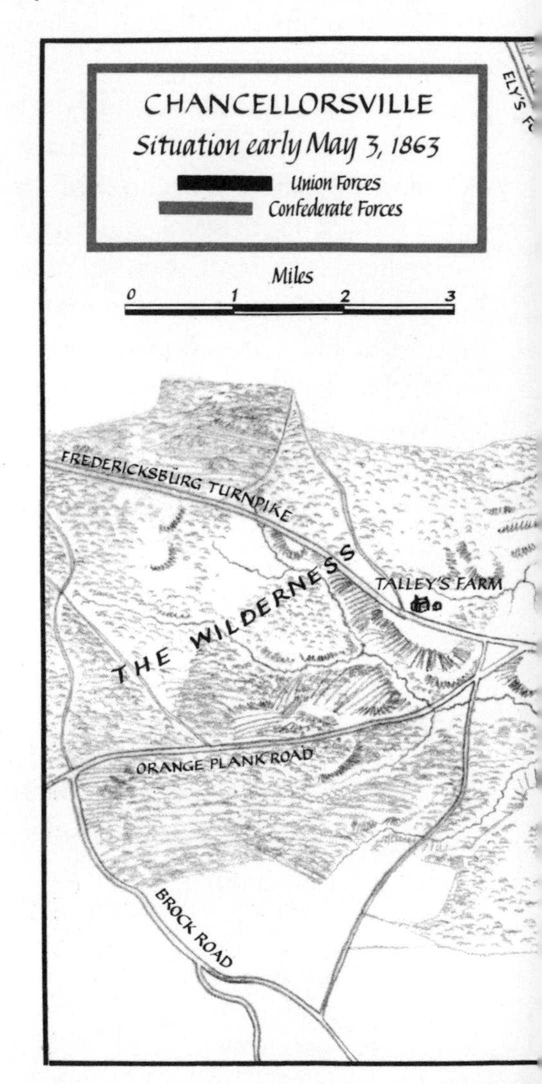

Handsome, bearded, brave Jeb Stuart struck with all his strength. Quickly capitalizing on Hooker's blunder, the new leader of the Confederate II Corps seized Hazel Grove, only one mile west of Chancellorsville, and mounted thirty-one guns. The Rebels could now sweep the open plain around the crossroads and batter Griffin at Fairview Cemetery.

"*Remember Jackson and Charge!*"

There can be no doubt that Mrs. Chesnut's opinion of Jackson was correct: he did indeed fire the hearts of his

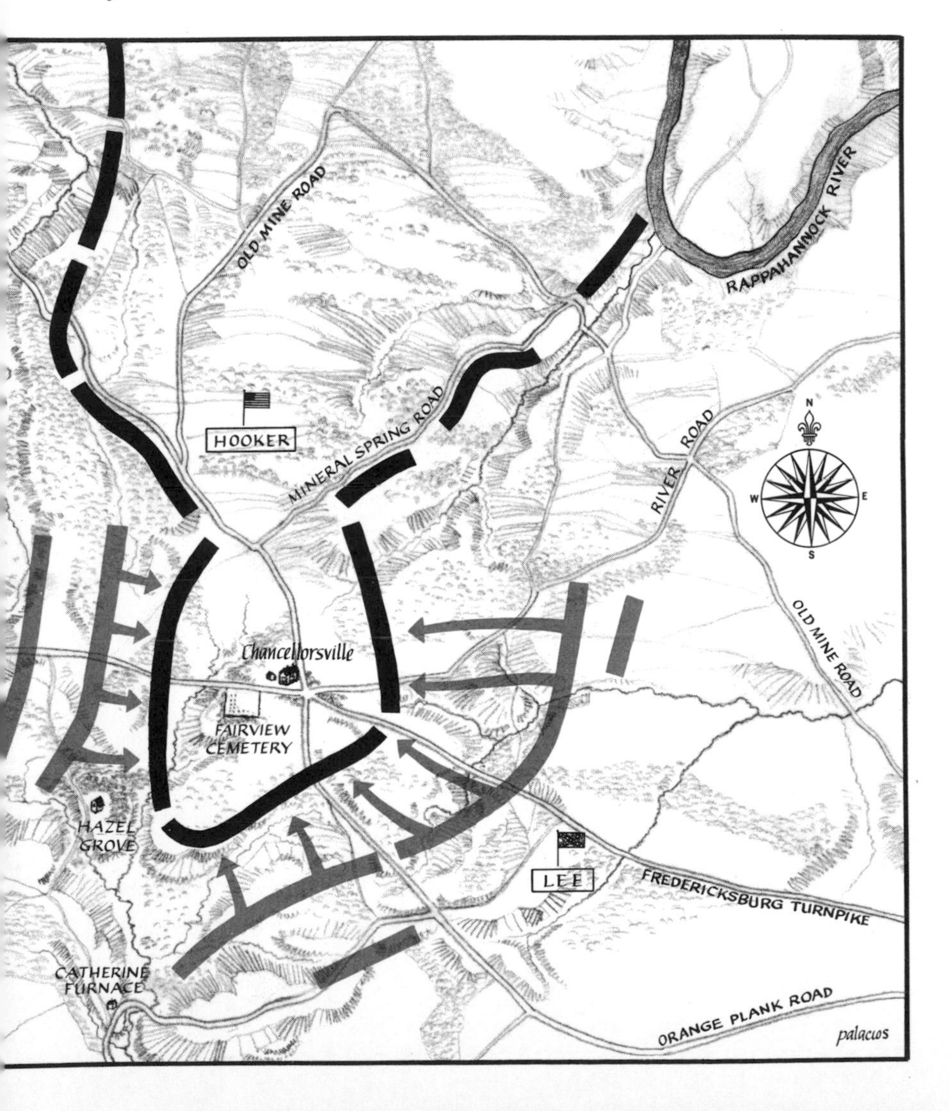

soldiers. The Confederate officers and men respected and admired Robert E. Lee. They called him The Old Tycoon and Marse Robert or Marse Bob, although never to his face or in his hearing. But they loved Stonewall Jackson. He drove them hard but praised them often. He had taught them to expect to win. On May 3, the II Corps went to battle crying, "Remember Jackson and charge!" Perhaps they already sensed that Stonewall would never lead them again.

The stout brigades rushed forward, firing at will, their bayonets fixed and battle banners rolling above the gunsmoke. They stormed the Union lines and were slammed back by the grim Federal defenders.

Stuart galloped up and down the line, conferring, encouraging, dodging solid shot and stray bullets. He sent the II Corps into attack a second time to tear at the Union flank. Survivors of the battle that day remembered their cavalier commander singing in a scornful baritone: "Old Joe Hooker, won't you come out of the wilderness?"

The tune was the popular "The Old Gray Mare, She Ain't What She Used to Be." Perhaps the little song was just the proper touch of reckless defiance and jaunty confidence. If old Joe Hooker wouldn't come out on his own, the II Corps would drive him out with shot, shell, and cold steel.

Griffin's Federal gunners, blackened by powder as smiths at a forge, swabbed the cannon muzzles, loaded, and fired. Shrapnel rained down from Fairview Cemetery. The Rebels formed up a third time and attacked again.

Full Fury of Battle

The men of both armies fought all morning with the strength of rage, inspiration, and madness. Rarely in the entire war between the states did battle fury rise to such a wild pitch and hold there so long. The Army of Northern Virginia endured punishing enfilade fire from the Northern guns and hurled their smoke-blackened bodies through the

Sunday, May 3: The Union and Confederate armies clash on the field of battle (drawing by Edwin Forbes).

smoldering woods at the Union lines. The Army of the Potomac stood for hours, as if the men were nailed to the earth. Their rifle barrels grew so hot they blistered the soldiers' hands. They bashed back the Rebel assaults all along their clumsy, curved line. Through the smoky din that hung in the trees, the Rebel yell and the answering curses ripped like the blood cry of fiends.

Fairview Cemetery

The focal spot of the third Rebel attack was Fairview Cemetery and Griffin's guns. The Confederates stormed the defense perimeter. Their battle banners jerked forward, and the color-bearers jammed the staffs into the torn sod between the gun pits and gravestones. The Union cannon blasted. The banners tossed and went down. Running blue figures scattered over the ground, turning to kneel and fire into the dense smoke.

Stuart's cannon at Hazel Grove wheeled and fired. Turf and tombstones scattered in fragments. The Federal infantry fell back. Teams of horses galloped to save the Union guns. The Rebel banners jerked up again, bent forward, and stayed aloft.

The Union line, breeched at the cemetery, contracted like a spasm, the convulsion of agony. Now the Rebels made a continuous advance more than five hundred yards forward all along the twisted front. General Wright and Generals Anderson and McLaws saw their platoons blend with the brigades from Alabama, Georgia, and North Carolina. The troops were tangled, but they were together! Both prongs of the Army of Northern Virginia had jabbed through and joined!

A Fallen General, a Shattered Army

One of Stuart's guns at Hazel Grove blasted, and a solid shot hissed across the sky. The ten-pound cannon ball smacked the portico of John Chancellor's big square red house, now General Hooker's headquarters. A wooden porch column wrenched loose from the impact and struck down the commander of the Army of the Potomac.

General Hooker sprawled unconscious, injured in the side and head. His staff officers rushed to him through a cloud of paint flakes, dust, and flying splinters. More solid shot and shells came crashing down. The house was struck repeatedly. The right wing of the Union army was giving way, and the center was buckling.

Like Stonewall Jackson, General Hooker was carried to the rear, wounded and bleeding. General Darius Couch took over command.

By 10 A.M., the woods and outworks of the Union defense line around Chancellorsville were burning, filling the air with thick, pungent smoke. Still the Confederates came on from the cemetery and across the Orange Plank Road. The flaming thickets and the dark pall spread over the forest seemed the funeral pyre of the Army of the Potomac.

General Couch ordered a general withdrawal to the Min-

Union General Darius Couch

eral Spring Road which covered the fords across the river north of Chancellorsville. Griffin, still manning the Federal guns, agreed to cover the retreat.

"I'll make 'em think hell isn't half a mile off!" he growled.

Triumph at Chancellorsville Clearing

From Hazel Grove, General Lee rode northeast through the debris of battle—wrecked cannon and overturned ammunition caissons, breeched fortifications, ripped tents, dying horses, scattered blankets, ammunition boxes, and rations. From the burning woods came the screams of trapped Union and Confederate wounded.

In the center of Chancellorsville clearing, the big red house burned like a victory bonfire. It was high noon.

Throngs of gray infantry from all the brigades and divisions clambered over the scorched, abandoned earthworks, congratulating each other. The Yankees were running for the river. As Lee rode into the clearing, his men, wild with jubilation at their great victory, exploded into the greatest demonstration of affection ever made in his presence. Colonel Charles C. Marshall, one of Lee's staff officers, described the scene:

"The fierce soldiers with their faces blackened with the smoke of battle, the wounded crawling with feeble limbs from the fury of the devouring flames, all seemed possessed of a common impulse. One long, unbroken cheer . . . rose high above the roar of battle, and hailed the presence of the victorious chief. He sat in the full realization of all that soldiers dream of—triumph . . . in the complete fruition of the success which his genius, courage, and confidence in his army had won. . . . It must have been from such a scene that men in ancient times rose to the dignity of gods."

CHRONOLOGY

JANUARY 1, 1863. As the new year begins, the Northern grasp of key points necessary to the survival of the enemy Confederate States of America threatens to become a strangle hold. Patrolling Union warships block many Southern ports, cutting off the supply of vital goods. The lower end of the Mississippi River, including the city of New Orleans, is held by a Federal army, and at the upper end of the Mississippi the citadel city of Vicksburg is beseiged by another Union force.

Southerners everywhere hope for a dazzling victory to prompt intercession by England, an end to the war, and independence.

JANUARY 26. President Abraham Lincoln appoints "Fighting Joe" Hooker to replace General Ambrose Burnside as commander of the Army of the Potomac.

JANUARY–APRIL 29. Confederate commander Robert E. Lee fortifies the Rebel defenses on the banks of the Rappahannock River at Fredericksburg, Virginia. Lee's army, short of food and basic supplies, endures a severe winter.

Across the river, General Hooker organizes the Army of the Potomac for a spring offensive, winning the confidence of his veteran troops and grudging praise from his officers.

APRIL 29. General George Stoneman's Federal cavalry pushes across the Rappahannock west of Fredericksburg. Hooker crosses at Kelly's Ford with three army corps and advances toward the Confederates.

Lee commands General Robert Anderson's division to stall the powerful Union drive.

Rain falls as the Army of the Potomac halts for the night.

APRIL 30, 2:30 P.M. Lee orders Anderson's troops to construct field fortifications—the first to be built in America.

NIGHT. General Stonewall Jackson's Confederate II Corps and a division under General Lafayette McLaws march west under cover of darkness to reinforce Anderson.

General Jubal Early, with 10,000 men and 45 cannons, remains at Fredericksburg to oppose any movement across the river by Union General John M. Sedgwick.

MAY 1, AFTERNOON. As the Rebels move west to meet him, Hooker nervously halts his army and fortifies the area around the Chancellorsville crossroads.

General Oliver O. Howard fails to anchor the Union right flank, leaving his XI Corps exposed and vulnerable to attack.

SUNSET AND EVENING. General Jeb Stuart's Rebel troops battle with General Henry Slocum's men at the Federal center.

NIGHT. Stuart discovers Howard's XI Corps "up in the air" and reports back to Confederate headquarters.

Two of Jackson's staff, Major Hotchkiss and Mr. Lacy, find a perfect route for a surprise attack on Howard: an abandoned cart track which flanks the Federal position.

Jackson proposes a massive assault on the XI Corps, leaving Lee with only Anderson's and McLaws' divisions. Lee agrees to divide his army a second time and gamble on victory.

MAY 2, 7:00 A.M. Jackson advances toward the Union right flank with 26,000 men. The troops of his second in command, General Ambrose P. Hill, serve as a rear guard.

MID-MORNING. Anderson's and McLaws' divisions are spread thinly at the center, but must hold there until Jackson can attack. Lee, uneasy, warns Confederate President Jefferson Davis that position and numbers greatly favor the Yankee invaders.

EARLY AFTERNOON. Union General Daniel Sickles probes for Confederate movement, opening a gap between his division and Howard's corps.

LATE AFTERNOON. Lee receives notice that Jackson, supported by Stuart, is nearly ready to attack. Yankee assaults, although not in massive strength, continue to threaten Anderson and McLaws.

Bad news comes to Lee from Fredericksburg. Confused by a twisted order Early has abandoned the earthworks there, opening the Confederate rear to attack by Sedgwick's Federal forces. Lee quickly orders Early to return to Fredericksburg, taking care not to alarm the rest of his soldiers.

5:15 P.M. Jackson strikes. His assault brigades overwhelm the unsuspecting Union XI Corps, inflicting 2,000 casualties. Griffin's artillery checks the Rebel assault. Confused by the sudden darkness, both sides halt and fix new positions. The Yankees' line is bent back, but not broken.

9:30 P.M. Stonewall Jackson, planning a night attack to encircle Hooker's army, rides forward to view his own lines. Suddenly he is shot down—by his own men—wounded three times.

10:00 P.M. to 2:00 A.M. MAY 3. Jackson is taken to a field hospital where his left arm is amputated. With Hill also wounded, command of the Confederate II Corps falls to Stuart, who has never before directed infantry movements.

MAY 3, 2:30 A.M. Lee learns of the disaster in the dark and laments the loss of Jackson. He orders Stuart to attack in the early morning, while Anderson's and McLaws' divisions try to force through the Union lines at Chancellorsville.

EARLY MORNING. Hooker orders Sedgwick to take Fredericksburg and then march to Chancellorsville. Through lack of confidence Hooker does not order the full-scale counterattack that might have brought him victory.

Stuart, Anderson, and McLaws attack Hooker on all sides. Stuart seizes Hazel Grove and drives the Federal artillery from Fairview Cemetery after a furious fight.

MID-MORNING. The two-pronged Rebel attack joins. General Hooker is wounded at his headquarters by a falling pillar. Hooker's second in command, General Darius Couch, orders Chancellorsville abandoned. Lee is cheered at Chancellorsville clearing by his victorious troops.

NOON. Sedgwick occupies Fredericksburg and attempts to drive on to meet with Hooker. He is stopped at Salem Church by Early, supported by McLaws.

MAY 4. With heavy casualties and ammunition shortages hampering his pursuit of Hooker, Lee goes to Salem Church to direct the attack on Sedgwick. The Union General slips his force away from the weary Rebels and retreats across the river.

MAY 5. Hooker orders a general withdrawal of the Army of the Potomac.

President Lincoln receives news of the Union rout.

Lee realizes he has not achieved the total victory he had hoped for.

MAY 7. Stonewall Jackson suddenly contracts pneumonia.

MAY 10. Jackson dies.

MAY 11–16. Jackson's funeral procession is held in Richmond. His body lies in state at the Confederate Capitol. Newspapers express the South's great sense of loss. The Rebels feel despair and defeatism for the first time.

MAY 16–31. Lee reorganizes the Army of Northern Virginia and plans his own fateful summer offensive north to Maryland and Pennsylvania.

Part Four

SALEM CHURCH and Afterward

Final Action at Salem Church

On May 3, while Lee and Stuart were smashing Hooker's main force, sturdy General Sedgwick had launched his own two-pronged attack on the Confederate troops at Fredericksburg. Twice his troops stormed Marye's Heights, where Burnside had been defeated the previous December. Another group of Union infantry and artillery slipped downriver two miles and attacked the flank of the Rebel defense.

Jubal Early's defenders beat back two assaults on the important earthworks, but under enfilade fire from the east, they withdrew in good order. Fighting a steady holding action, Early moved his outnumbered force back toward Lee. The Federals pushing after him seemed puzzled and hesitant, as though lack of confidence had spread from Hooker's main force like an infection. The two groups sparred and shifted around the Orange Plank Road at another insignificant spot on the maps called Salem Church.

Beyond the burning house at Chancellorsville, Hooker's troops reeled back north and braced themselves again along the Mineral Spring Road. There they re-formed and waited to fend off Lee's death stroke.

Although Hooker's army offered only sporadic stiff resistance, Lee's divisions were too exhausted to destroy the cramped Federal force. Something had to be done to help Early, who could not be expected to hold out too long against Sedgwick, now positioned in the Rebel rear. As he had done before, Lee detached McLaws for reinforcement

LEFT: *Confederate General Jubal Early.* RIGHT: *Confederate General Lafayette McLaws*

and rescue. Fortunately, the marching distance was short. McLaws's men reached Early in the late afternoon. From the roof of a tobacco barn McLaws watched four Rebel brigades bloody Sedgwick's divisions. The Federals were repulsed, and the action dwindled with darkness.

Although Georgia-born Lafayette McLaws was the ranking Confederate Major General in term of service, and Jubal Early the most recently promoted, it was McLaws who now asked for suggestions, and the younger man who gave them. The weary Confederates were drawn in a rough semicircle around Sedgwick. Early advocated an attack from the left, preceded by an artillery bombardment. The plan depended heavily on McLaws's full cooperation.

But McLaws hesitated. The territory around Salem

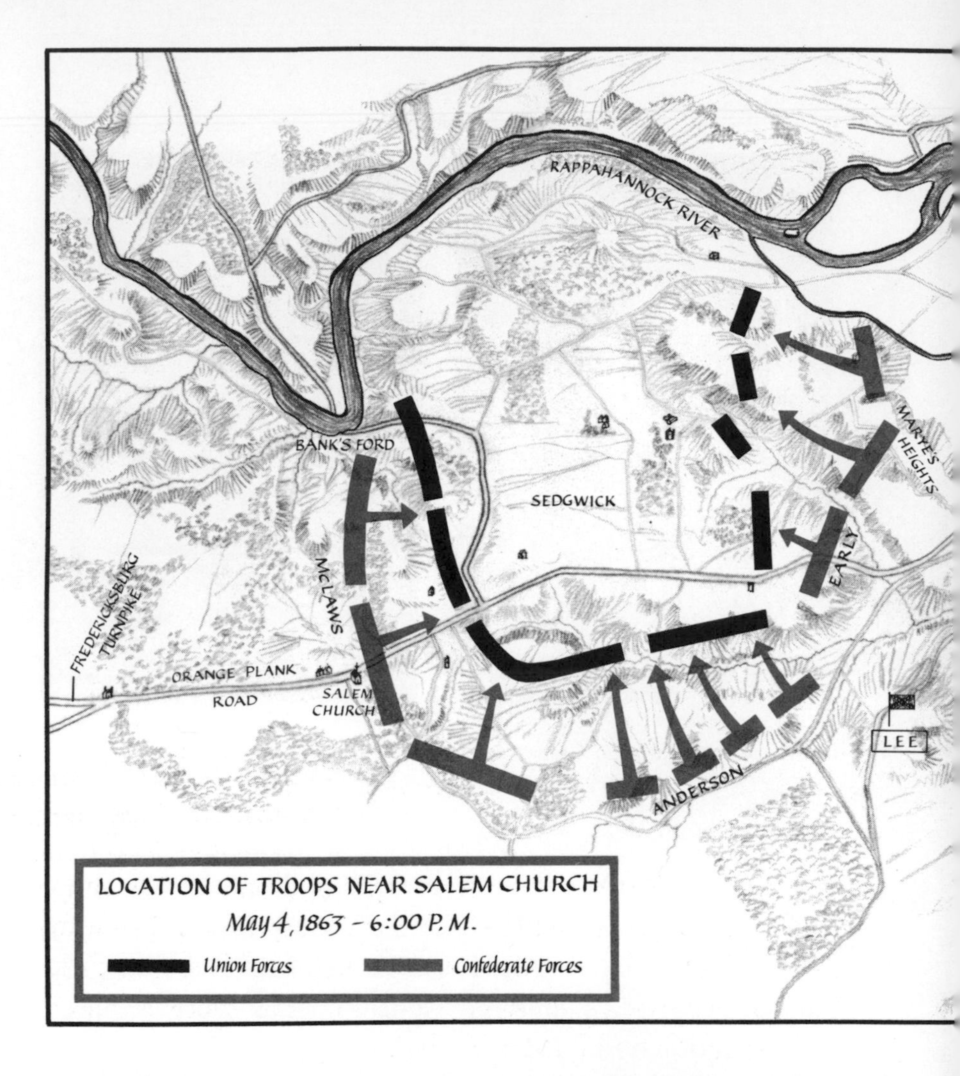

Church was unfamiliar to him and Sedgwick's artillery seemed as good as Griffin's guns. Moreover, he knew Anderson's troops were on the way. He suggested that Early start the assault.

About 11 A.M. on May 4, Anderson reported to McLaws near Salem Church. Before any decision was made, Lee arrived. He came after reluctantly breaking off pursuit of Hooker north of Chancellorsville.

The afternoon dragged slowly. The tired Rebels maneu-

vered sluggishly, forcing themselves. It was close to six o'clock when the carefully positioned Confederate artillery at last opened fire. After a good start, nothing went well. Brigades blundered together and again, night fell too soon for success. Sedgwick, under cover of darkness, slipped away. The glum, exhausted Confederates slumped in the woods and listened to Federal boots beating like a giant drum roll on the pontoon bridges that led back north to safety. Unable to join with Hooker south of the Rappahannock, Sedgwick fell back across Bank's Ford—the very spot his superior was to have opened for him two days earlier.

The support-and-attack action that saved Early and Fredericksburg also saved Hooker, for Lee, without strong reinforcements still, could not strike the finishing blow, the *coup de grâce.*

Hooker Retreats—May 5–6

General Hooker lay dazed. At times he woke from what appeared to his staff to be a deep sleep. His comments and questions were sometimes vague, incoherent. The falling pillar seemed to have stunned his mind as well as battering and bruising his body.

All his "perfect" plans had gone wrong. A large portion of his mighty army had never seen battle; yet he had squandered 17,000 men and had been routed in two different places by forces half the size of his own.

On May 5, Fighting Joe Hooker ordered a general withdrawal of the Army of the Potomac. Lee's battle-weary army could offer only weak pursuit. Stuart's artillery had exhausted the supply of shells and solid shot; the Rebel gunners were forced to fire hunks of railroad rails at the retreating Federal columns. The blue army limped away. The battle at Chancellorsville was over.

Confederate Losses

For all the brilliance and daring of the days of battle, Lee's gallant, outnumbered army had suffered greatly and had achieved less than the total victory the Rebel commander and the Confederate government and citizens had hoped for. The

Confederate war prisoners captured at Chancellorsville

dazzling series of marches and assaults would be studied by officers in training all over the world for decades to come, but the losses in the tangled woods were wounds from which the Army of Northern Virginia would never recover.

The Rebels lost 13,000 men in the rout of the Yankee foe. Lee's army lay maimed and feeble in the smoldering forest, too weak to exploit what they had so gloriously won. No problem had been solved; many problems had merely been delayed. The English Parliament might be impressed by the victory, but not enough to come to the rescue of the Confederacy. So long as the Army of the Potomac was still intact, Lincoln could use it, without drawing on his western forces under General Rosecrans in Tennessee and grim General Grant at Vicksburg. Lee had brilliantly won a breathing spell, but at terrible cost.

In the meantime, at Guinea Station, Stonewall Jackson lay dying.

A Telegram to Lincoln

Curiously enough, General Hooker had not kept his President well-informed. Vague reports had reached the White House that all was going more or less as planned. So on the morning of May 6, the President was stunned by the telegram that reached him. The Army of the Potomac had been driven back across the Rappahannock to Falmouth.

Gray with despair, Lincoln paced back and forth, clutching the flimsy copy sheet. He shook his head and said over and over, "My God, my God, what will the country say! What will the country say!"

"*God Will Not Take Him*"

Jackson lay in a small bedroom at the Chandler farm. He had responded quite well after the amputation of his shattered limb. On May 6, General Lee had sent him a message:

"Tell him to make haste and get well, and come back to me as soon as he can. He has lost his left arm; but I have lost my right arm."

Stonewall smiled slightly at the flattering remark. His wife and daughters had been able to join him, and he was well attended by skillful doctors. He felt he would recover. He would be Lee's "right arm" still. There were hammer blows to be struck.

But on May 7, Jackson's rugged frame was attacked by pneumonia. A specialist was summoned, but the fever mounted, and the general slipped in and out of delirium.

The officers and men of the Army of Northern Virginia

held special gatherings to pray for Jackson's recovery. Lee knelt in his own tent. He said to his worried staff, his voice touched with desperation, "Surely, General Jackson must recover; God will not take him from us, now that we need him so much."

"Let Us Cross the River"

May 10, 1863, was a beautiful spring Sunday. Jackson lay still, breathing slowly, harshly, his congested lungs laboring. His wife and family, staff officers, and doctors watched helplessly.

Jackson's mind flickered with memories and visions of the advance against the Union right flank. He rasped, "Order A. P. Hill to prepare for action. . . . Pass the infantry to the front!"

His forehead was slick with perspiration.

In the early afternoon, his wife and her brother, Lieutenant Morrison, read aloud from the Bible and sang a hymn, "Show Pity, Lord." Choking spasms shook Jackson's body, although between them he rested quietly. He fought stubbornly against the delirium that caused him to mutter about orders and battle formations.

He rallied once, twice, three times, struggling up out of unconsciousness to request that he be buried in the family plot at Lexington, Virginia.

The clock in the parlor struck three. A soft, scented breeze rustled the lilacs outside the open bedroom window. Each tortured breath rattled in his throat. Fifteen more minutes.

"Let us cross over the river and rest under the shade of the trees," he said quietly.

Then, Stonewall Jackson was dead.

"A Great National Calamity Has Befallen Us"

Jackson's body, dressed in civilian clothes and wrapped in a dark blue military overcoat, was placed in a glass-topped coffin and shipped by train to Richmond. All the grieving city turned out in solemn ceremony.

Church bells tolled, flags hung at half-mast, and guns boomed every sixty seconds. All business stopped, government offices closed, and thousands stood bareheaded as the hearse, covered with evergreen sprays and wreaths of flowers, rolled by. The pallbearers were all general officers. President Jefferson Davis rode in an open carriage, and the members of the Confederate Cabinet followed on foot, two by two. There were black plumes everywhere, a riderless horse, and the thud of muffled drums.

More thousands came to pay their respects while Jackson's body lay in state in the Capitol building.

Mrs. Chesnut knelt by the flower- and flag-decked bier and later wrote in her diary, "Shall I ever forget the pain and fear of it all—to see Stonewall Jackson lying in state at the Capitol!"

Robert E. Lee's words mingled resignation and a sense of tragic loss: "I know not how to replace him. God's will be done. I trust He will raise up someone in his place."

President Jefferson Davis summed up the feelings of a grief-stricken, despairing nation: "A great national calamity has befallen us."

In the months after Jackson's death, the attitude of the Southern nation-at-arms underwent a corroding change. Militant confidence in the Confederate armies gave way to loss of heart and slowly, finally, to resignation and helplessness. The most glorious victory of the war seemed hollow some-

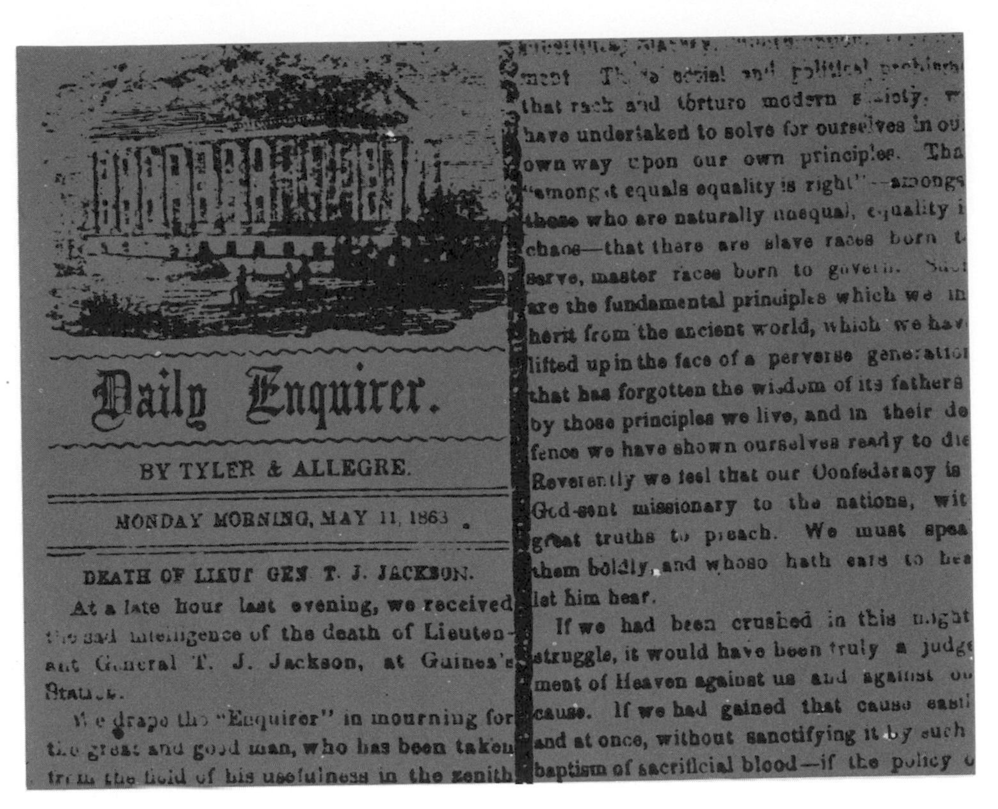

Daily Enquirer.

BY TYLER & ALLEGRE.

MONDAY MORNING, MAY 11, 1863.

DEATH OF LIEUT GEN T. J. JACKSON.

At a late hour last evening, we received the sad intelligence of the death of Lieutenant General T. J. Jackson, at Guinea's Station.

We drape the "Enquirer" in mourning for the great and good man, who has been taken from the field of his usefulness in the zenith

...ment. The social and political problems that rack and torture modern society we have undertaken to solve for ourselves in our own way upon our own principles. That "amongst equals equality is right"—amongst those who are naturally unequal, equality is chaos—that there are slave races born to serve, master races born to govern. Such are the fundamental principles which we inherit from the ancient world, which we have lifted up in the face of a perverse generation that has forgotten the wisdom of its fathers by those principles we live, and in their defence we have shown ourselves ready to die. Reverently we feel that our Confederacy is a God-sent missionary to the nations, with great truths to preach. We must speak them boldly, and whoso hath ears to hear let him hear.

If we had been crushed in this mighty struggle, it would have been truly a judgement of Heaven against us and against our cause. If we had gained that cause easily and at once, without sanctifying it by such baptism of sacrificial blood—if the policy of

Editorial in a Richmond paper the day after Jackson's death

how, spoiled by the death of Jackson. Without him, many felt there was no end in sight but slow, inevitable defeat. Final loss could be delayed, blows could be parried and given, but they would be desperate measures undertaken by a dying nation. The cost of the victory at Chancellorsville had been too great. The Confederacy was doomed.

Years later, a minister prayed over the granite monument at Lexington, Virginia:

"When in Thy inscrutable wisdom, Oh Lord, Thou didst ordain that the Confederacy should fall, then Thou didst find it necessary to remove Thy servant, Stonewall Jackson. Amen."

Reorganization of the Army of Northern Virginia

One year would pass before the Army of the Potomac would again venture south into Virginia and attempt to seize Richmond. Then it would be directed by General Ulysses S. Grant, who had crushed the Rebel defenses at Vicksburg.

The situation was perilous. Lee warned the Richmond government that Confederate forces were too thin. Some one would have to decide between Mississippi and Virginia. It was impossible to save both; yet the states in rebellion could not afford to lose either.

After some discussion and gnawing delay, the Rebel armies in the west were left to fight the Union forces of Generals Grant and Rosecrans unaided. Lee's Army of Northern Virginia was brought up to full strength by returning to it the commands of Generals Longstreet, Hood, and Pickett. The 12,000 men they led had been absent from Chancellorsville. If those crack divisions had been on the field, the course of American history might have changed. An armistice might have been signed on the banks of the Rappahannock instead of two years later at Appomattox Court House. But after any crucial battle there are "might have beens."

By the end of May, 1863, Lee had gathered nearly 75,000 men. Longstreet, Hill, and another of Jackson's earlier subordinates, Richard S. Ewell, were given corps command. Neither Hill nor Ewell ever equaled the brilliance and success of their dead master.

Lee turned again to his planned offensive against the North. If he had won as he had wished at Chancellorsville, it would not have been necessary. But now he planned to move into Maryland and Pennsylvania, drawing Hooker after him. Such a move would force Lincoln's administration to protect Washington. Federal plans, both in the east and west, would be disrupted. During the summer, the Confederate army could live off the fat farmlands of the North and gather in much-needed supplies by raiding Union storage depots.

The attack, Lee indicated quite clearly, could not and should not be considered an invasion, but rather a prolonged raid that might well cause the loud voices in the North already raised for peace to convince stubborn President Lincoln. Such a raid, too, might cause General Hooker, still commanding, to expose the Army of the Potomac just once more. And then . . .

The Road to Gettysburg

The battle of Chancellorsville had given the Army of Northern Virginia proof of what it had long believed—that it could beat the Army of the Potomac decisively. The fight that raged in the woods indicated that Mr. Lincoln still had not found a general with Lee's habit of winning.

Because of what had happened at Chancellorsville, the two armies would meet again at Gettysburg, Pennsylvania, in the greatest battle of the Civil War, but the Army of the Potomac would be directed by General George Meade. The Army of Northern Virginia would still be commanded by Robert E. Lee.

But there in the north, there would be no lightning assault by the Confederate II Corps, no hammer blow to batter the Federal forces, no victory at Gettysburg; for the General who had helped Lee most at Chancellorsville—Stonewall Jackson—had died at the Rappahannnock, his death a disaster in victory.

A pontoon bridge like the ones that carried Hooker's army back across the Rappahannock to safety

FOR FURTHER READING

Nonfiction

ANGLE, PAUL M. and EARL S. MIERS. *The Tragic Years: 1860–1865.* 2 vols. New York: Simon and Schuster, 1960.

BRADFORD, GAMALIEL. *Lee the American.* Boston: Houghton Mifflin, 1927.

CATTON, BRUCE. *The Army of the Potomac: Mr. Lincoln's Army.* New York: Doubleday, 1962.

———. *The Centennial History of the Civil War.* Vol. 2 *Terrible Swift Sword.* Vol. 3 *Never Call Retreat.* New York: Doubleday, 1963, 1965.

CHESNUT, MARY BOYKIN. *A Diary from Dixie.* Boston: Houghton Mifflin, 1961.

DOUGLAS, HENRY KYD. *I Rode with Stonewall.* Chapel Hill: University of North Carolina Press, 1940.

DOWDY, CLIFFORD. *The Land They Fought For.* New York: Doubleday, 1955.

FREEMAN, DOUGLAS SOUTHALL. *Lee's Lieutenants.* 2 vols. New York: Charles Scribners Sons, 1943.

———. *R. E. Lee, A Biography.* 4 vols. New York: Scribner's, 1944.

WILLIAMS, T. HARRY. *Lincoln and His Generals.* New York: Knopf, 1958.

Fiction

BENÉT, STEPHEN VINCENT. *John Brown's Body.* New York: Rinehart, 1928.

CRANE, STEPHEN. *The Red Badge of Courage.* New York: Macmillan, 1895.

KANTOR, MACKINLAY. *Andersonville.* New York: World, 1955.

MITCHELL, MARGARET. *Gone with the Wind.* New York: Macmillan, 1939.

PALMER, BRUCE. *Many Are the Hearts.* New York: Simon and Schuster, 1961.

INDEX

INDEX

Bloom

1L+

30p.